singular methodology one

sean::adrian::brijbasi

Published simultaneously in the United States
and Great Britain in 2026
by Pretend Genius
Copyright © Sean::Adrian::Brijbasi

This book is copyright under the Berne Convention
No reproduction without permission
All rights reserved

ISBN: 9798985908947

other books by Sean::Adrian::Brijbasi

One Note Symphonies
for Emma

Still Life in Motion
for those who play
Marius and Andréus

The Unknowed Things
for Julius

The Dictionary of Coincidences, Volume i
for Emma

S{E}AN?
for EM{M}A+

E{M}MA+ the ghost orchids
for Emma

darling two hearts
for E{M}MA+ the ghost orchids

Stories for Nadira
*for Adrian, Andréus, Elijah, Helena, Julius,
Marius, Nadira*

Play Championship World-Class
Tennis with Bjorn McEnroe
*for Adrian, Andréus, Elijah, Helena, Julius,
Marius, Nadira*

The World That Destroyed the World
*for Adrian, Andréus, Elijah, Helena, Julius,
Marius, Nadira*

The Book of Lashonda
*for Adrian, Andréus, Elijah, Helena, Julius,
Marius, Nadira*

ENTROPALACE
for my brother Troy

NO ONE CAN SEE THE WORLD I LIVE IN

for the only one

M.A.R.I.A.201001000

for my sister Simone

Bend. Human Willing.

for Emma

Vita enim mortuorum in memoria vivorum est posita.

—MTC

an ordered composition	1
singular methodology one	9
a brief pregenesis	17
further suppositions	27
somewhere else from where it started	35
kind to her	45
panther lily	57
the history of an empire	67
nightkeeper	77
a dark forgetfulness	87
our simple biology	93
it was all	101

an ordered composition

1. There's a grave dug into my body. In the middle of my chest. A perfectly shaped rectangular prism. The skin smooth all around. I've wondered what to bury there. Something that would keep its meaning for as long as I lived. A poem torn from a book. A letter I had saved. A photograph. Or something more elusive. Something that existed only in the mirrors and windows around me. Something fleeting.

2. Then cover the grave with a piece of fabric. The same color as my skin. Leave it unmarked so no one would notice. If, for example, I was at the beach or playing tennis without a shirt. Unless, forgetting my grave. I moved in such a way as to partly open the covering. Like a poorly closed envelope might be opened. After

being thrown onto a table. And inside an invitation to look more closely.

3. The movement would be sudden. A quick turn. Caused by surprise. A leap to avoid a rain puddle. Caused by happiness. Falling backwards onto a bed. Caused by exhaustion. The types of sudden movements are few while the causes of sudden movements are many. I believed the covering would be undone by a leap. If the leap was caused by happiness or from some necessity related to survival—to not fall into a deep chasm, for example—I couldn't be sure.

4. To live for a hundred years. To wring everything out of that living until the end. Or to live for weeks a hundred times over. To walk with the first sapiens. To bury the first dead pharaoh. To peek through the

window at the woman posing for Leonardo. To see the painting of the woman hanging on the wall of a museum in a city on a planet wandering the Orion Nebula. And there in the atrium of the museum, a piano. Someone playing music I hadn't heard for a thousand years.

5. The idea of message would still exist. The means of sending one, however, currently unknown. The person making song. The outflow of sound over several minutes. But the end of sound leading to sound instead of silence from which perception is borne. Tedious. Mind-numbing. Humans. Tiring but loved all the same. And then in all the chatter I hear a new word. For the feeling of an expected moment that never arrives.

6. It's all going away from me now. I hear the piano in my sleep. Notes played of an ordered composition. A glass of water I had placed on the windowsill the night before. I can see the sky through its lens, but I can't find the sun from any angle.

7. I hear the turning of carriage wheels and the clapping of horse hooves come to a stop on the cobblestones in front of our house. Someone is visiting. A woman of a particular mind. I'll miss the beauty of her arrival. How she walks through. How she lingers. How the breeze wants to. And then does.

8. I'll take great care to rise because the covering on my grave is not fastened tight. I see the woman in the glass picture frames as she travels the room. She moves in a distinct trajectory. I calculate her destination to the photograph of pigeons.

Her image there among them. Their flight stilled under an evening sun. But she pauses inside the photograph of the grave. When the flowers were still fresh. Changed many times over since. I hope she doesn't feel it. As if it were that first day.

9. She lingers there as one might. Then finally moves. Her hair trails behind her as a breeze blows through the room. But enough time passes to know she has gone. The pigeons mid-flight alone. The windows transparent clear. The horse starts up. The carriage wheels make their first turn. But my eyes stay on the name. And the dates on the gravestone instead. The epitaph too thinly etched to see from here. But I remember it. Words I can't forget: *unable are the loved to die*. From a poet. A long time ago read.

10. The woman said something to me once. I want her to say it again. I want to bury what she said in my grave. I'll chase her. From train window to drinking glass. From hand mirror to long mirror. From deep lake to fast-moving river. I'll see into the trees. Search drops of rain diffused on leaves. I'll catch her. And she'll tell me. I'll keep it close. My buried treasure. And as such. Something beautiful to be heard. But something that no one will hear.

i: waking

He enters before dawn.

The lantern catches dust.

The horse is already awake.

And shifts its weight.

From one hoof to another.

The water bucket is half full.

And colder than the air.

singular methodology one

11. I follow the sound of the carriage. Across the paths between us. Created at an always current time. Some hidden by the uncut grass. Bent faintly by the carriage wheel. As the carriage travels through the outdoor garden. In the shadows of the outdoor garden shadows of steel. And yet not bouncy. Its fibrous wood pronounced in soft cellular pathologies. A turn down pause-way fleeting avenue. And I the budding master. Of multiple singular methodologies.

12. Singular methodology one: a quick climb to the carriage-top for a brief pied-a-terre with the kings of inertia and the reigning queens of gravity. The air cuts. A form called the body is carved up. A form called the body bleeds. But the rain will come. And the raining cleans the cavity.

Thoughts leave unsaddled words. *Tempora mutantur. Vincit qui patitur.* As time travels with the wind. And the wind travels with the birds.

13. Shall I peek down from up here? My head through the open carriage window. My neck stretched beyond all but a few's comprehension. I ask you to comprehend to make a few seconds of your next minute better. My neck stretched long to lay my cheek on her long sweater. Pulled down to just above her knees (and all the pulled-down-to-just-above-her-knees tension). A little cashmere but a lot more wool. I could be allergic. I could sneeze.

14. I'll stay on the carriage top. And think through her summer hat. When I rode a hansom of similar trot. Turning on what looked like White Allium wheels. On that

planet travelling the Orion Nebula. A needle stitch along the cut of a Persian cotton seam. I drank the water they made cold in jugs beneath a colding bough. Her summer hat. The one she played croquet in to keep the heat of the sun from her summer brow.

15. I'll wend my way through the interlace. Past the straw and crepe used to make fake flowers look real. And find her winter brow. So stark in comparison. I might love it more. If love for a brow could be so powerful. There are those who love her spring or autumn brow. But I'd put her winter brow in my grave. When once inside from the cold she takes off her hat to reveal her hair. And looks at me. I'll bury everything of that moment there.

16. She'll feel my thin biology on her skin. But she's too proper a lady to scratch in camera view. And hides her scratching— the edge of her thumb fingernail—in the formal hat removal she'll have to complete in strange company. And in doing so make me real.

17. But beauty is too close to death to stay in one place too long. We'll need respite to survive it. Like that moment when the record needle is picked up. And put down again. In the same place. In the same song. Time enough to pause. Time enough to breathe. Beauty is the absence of the oxygen we need. I'll catch for air. I'll freeze. Like when we played freeze tag. When all the others ran and I waited to be unfreezed.

18. So much to learn today. History and new equations. The transitive property of

geometry. The clockworks. The Zaza-Gorani. Though I never held my breath and sometimes didn't move even after I was set free. Unless touched by the hand of Maria.

ii: rising

He removes the blanket.

The horse's coat is warm underneath.

He brushes along the shoulder.

Then the flank.

Dust rises.

Hangs in the light and settles again.

He combs the tail once.

And straightens the mane.

By hand.

a brief pregenesis

19. The pigeons fly on either side of us like wings on the helmet of Mercury. As if they're lifting the earth and the roots in the earth. Softly from their loving dirt. I see your reflection in a passing carriage window and think we could be a couple. Your baby soul all beauty. My baby soul all muscle. Because some beauty is too unaware and gentle to protect itself. I follow the carriage tracks to the lake around which a mile could be perambled.

20. Animal memories rise from the water's surface as mist or other types of seasonal weather. Heat in summer. Ice crystals in winter. I see where those who have left the path have travelled. I see where the land is trampled. I walk up the stairs to the hilltop there and look back as you walk

down. I count five birds leave a tree across the way. I think about stirring my tea. With my left hand. The first time we meet. With my right hand. Another day.

21. From the building across the lake. A woman standing in an opened window. Keeps one foot in the space. Between the curtain hem and the floor. Feels the fabric descend from her ankle to her toes. Hears a knock on the apartment door. But doesn't open it. She's waiting for the man. She sees across the way. Turn and call out to the woman. She'll hear an echo. Though what name I say. She won't know.

22. But I don't call out. I only think her name. Maria. Fallen leaves scrape the path around my feet. The woman in the building sees. The five birds leave the

tree. Nearer for her. Further for me. And distracted by the arc of their flight. Loses sight of us. When she turns to look again. We've disappeared. The birds have gone too. And all that she's left with are the trees, the clouds, the sky, and the lake.

23. For a moment free from the idea of people. A brief pregenesis. Everywhere pregnant with becoming. She might have flown over here, her pupils dilating along the way, to murder me, if things had turned out differently. And I might have swum to the bottom of the lake to hide behind a lake stone until it was safe. A million years. A hundred million years. Before I returned to the surface to breathe the air of a thousand epochs.

24. Riverbed coins found in ocean waters. The imprints of bygone trees. Stirred up by another country's heavy sending.

Early afternoon sleep. Dreams of someone else's memories. My hand covers my face. My elbow bending. Still space enough for the afternoon breeze. For the curious child's eye to peek through. Like when the woman sees the horse-breath-puffs drift by the carriage curtain. Gone by the time they would have reached me. And calls out to the coachman from inside: faster.

25. And faster so the wind lifts my shirt. Uncovers my grave. Exposes the secret passageways hid beneath my skirt. Maybe the sweater wool will make her sneeze. Maybe my grave will catch her spit. Feel her mitosis inside my body. At least the start of it. The detachment of the first division. Brings me to my knees. The first syllable of the first world. Dropped from the first word. The first sound misheard.

The first image a mirage. A murmur resembles my name. And you. Or is it you? Looking my way. As I watch you give "the brushing" (*le brossage*) to the horse's mane.

26. From across the road. Then across the field. Across the river. Across a far-seeing-but-close-feeling space. If this is the end. I know it will happen only once. You hum a tune. I can't make out from here. Sing a song for a child and you can see it in their eyes. The sparkle like the lightest drizzle on the light-green park marble makes me brave. If this is the end. I know. It will happen only once.

27. But there's nowhere to use this bravery. In a moment it's gone. And just because you were brave once doesn't mean you'll be brave again. That could have been the last of it. I would have done everything

then. But she'll get it out of me once more. Once more after that. And once more yet. I'll take the runaway horse by the reins. I'll slow its breathing. Like she slows mine. Though I'll never show her how fast I breathe otherwise.

28. From thinking about her out there. And the dangers which life brings with it (in any case). But the horse is calm around her. I hope the world is too. And gives her time and space to grow beautiful. The way she's supposed to do. Young and ancient in a single body. To live her stories and tell them too. The carriage starts again. The sun shines through the trees. Along the riverside. Illuminates the road beneath their darkness. As far as we can see.

29. I hear her singing. Feel the bloom in my chest. Pushing up from my grave. I'll lie

still on the ground. Look up to the sky. She'll picnic around my body. The bee will visit. The butterfly. And slowly. From morning until night. My body will sink into the earth. Until only the flower remains above. And of the millions of them around her. I hope she picks mine. Keeps it in a vase of water for a time. And after it too dies. Presses it into a book I might have written. Only for her.

iii: catching

He lifts each hoof in order.

The mud comes away easy.

The shoes are tight.

And the nails sound.

The metal catches the lantern light.

He taps each shoe once.

And returns the tools to the wall.

further suppositions

30. At night when all the windows are quiet. And yesterday's newspaper is put in the fire. A carriage passes through the snowy night unheard. Leaves behind two straight lines. Along the road. And someone looking out. Might guess what passed through there. Make further suppositions. A coach of so-and-so size. Heading south—see how the tree branches are disturbed. And write on the window glass. Between those two carriage wheel lines. The name of the book: *Bend. Human Willing.*

31. Though by morning the tracks would be gone. Covered by snow. So that no one would know. What compelled anyone. To scribble those words. If they could see them. As the sun shined through. The name of a book. About someone lying in

a room. Her hair black. And straight as it ever was. Her face. Something similar. Reminding us of something that is the same. As it ever was.

32. Her skin cold but soon. The same temperature as the room. And the same temperature of all the other places. She'll go. And so the time comes again. When everything uninvited returns. And I'll hope—does it ever end?—to disappear. To a place where I can sleep. But not dream. Where not a sliver of life. Not a single photon of light intrudes. On this greatest sorrow.

33. There was a time when her hair was as disordered as her bookshelf. The tragedies of Aeschylus and Euripides sloped against children's books. Old schoolbooks pressed against primers on how to play world-class tennis or grow

bigger tomatoes. And then one day straight. Everything in its place. Ordered by genre and within genre by alphabet. And on the other side of the same wall a photograph of her face.

34. Looking toward the window across the room. The sun shining on that open space. Where I'll sit like the coachman and behind me my beautiful and sad passenger. Because everything beautiful is sad. The wind moving a few strands of her hair. Like someone pulling out a book from her perfectly ordered bookshelf. To read a few sentences and put it back misplaced. Or absent-mindedly leave one on the table or gloriously on the chair. For me to return and reorder. To comb it all back straight.

35. She, who couldn't stay long. Like a butterfly that disappeared but that left a

good memory in my heart. I've forgotten now. I'll retrace. All the steps I took to get here. The air before. Was it stale? What were those flowers? Did the curtains shift? Did her eyes behind me look perplexed when someone removed *The Dictionary of Coincidences, Volume I* from her bookshelf and left an empty space there?

36. Something could crawl inside to hide. Something could glide in. After being worn out. From beating its wings. Or drawn in by gravity. To a black space where a book used to be. Taking everything. Except the carriage and its lonely passenger. Travelling the cosmic terrain. The horse hooves silent on Orion's plain.

37. But in her head knocking endlessly. As if on a door that will never be opened. And me on the other side. Waving goodbye. To no one. To everyone. My body getting smaller. My light dimmer. As I recede into the void. And the void, in turn. Recedes into my grave. A perfectly shaped rectangular prism. In the middle of my chest.

iv: finding

He takes the harness from its hook.

The leather is cool.

He checks each buckle for cracks.

Finds none.

He sets the collar.

And adjusts the traces until they are even.

The sound of the metal on metal is clean.

The horse is patient.

somewhere else from where it started

38. The tiny apple tree has grown big. But the shade tree he climbed. As a child. Has been cut down. To make this piece of paper. On which a few words are scribbled. Scratched out but still legible. Directions for the coachman who said. He would commit them to memory. But when the road divided. And in that moment. As in all moments. Became "of two minds". And chose the wrong way.

39. Through the sugarcane field. Where the blood of his ancestors congealed. On the sugarcane field floor. To grow sweet sugar to put into the tea. I think about stirring. With my left hand. The first time we meet. With my right hand. Another day.

40. I had that dream of you again. Did you dream of me? Someone placed a rose on the piece of paper. That reminded him of his mother. Which made him forget the directions written there. And he either lost or found. His way. Everyday is a fight. Against the end. Of all things.

41. If I could find the wedding book. Someone signed. The year before I was born. *Felicitations and happy life. Beautiful couple. Beautiful wife.* She couldn't stay long. And left mid-ceremony. Heard the church organ behind her. Peeked from time to time to see. If she was followed by the town butterfly. Or the town bee. She's taking the forbidden path. To a secret house. Where someone who wasn't invited lived.

42. When should she take it? If not then. The carriage knows where to go. Along the length of the summer stream. She can hear it running. Like the first light of day. Moving over. The dark corners. Of her summer dream. Wake up. Wake up. The carriage is nearing the cemetery. She tells the coachman to stop. They almost went past it. Mist rises. From between the gravestones. She knows no one there.

43. But she can imagine it all. The hard earth. The concrete. The bending trees. The rough and calm. Wind and breeze. The sea churning. The hot and distant sun. The never-ending rain. The asteroids colliding. The universe expanding. The wake and wedding dance. How they cried. And laughed. How they loved. All those they met. By chance. She only wanted to stretch. Her legs. And walk

silently. For a minute or two. Among those. For whom a life well lived. Ended there.

44. I'll walk by the coachman. Feel the bridle scrape my leg. And into the carriage. Opening a long walk. As if through a train. To find the empty seat. Next to you. To rest my head. On your shoulder. And fall asleep. On the body. Of your neck. The precious vein. The warm blood pulsing. While you gaze. Through the window. Passing by rows of seats. And feel differently. Not the same person. I was when we boarded. Because as I get closer. I think. You're always in. The distance for me.

45. All these. Seats taken. Keep me moving. And this fast walking. Feels like wasted time. But I'll pass by. In slow motion if. I

see someone. Sitting next to you. Maybe someone has lain. Across the tracks. And the train will stop suddenly. I'll lose my balance and fall. Like I've always wanted to fall. And finally wake up from this sleepwalking. Please have a seat sir. If you don't find one now. We'll have to remove you.

46. The carriage. Doesn't make stops. At this or that grave. Lucky I have one here. In the middle of my chest. And I can keep going. As the train passes through the earth. The earth passes through the galaxy. And the galaxy like billions of other galaxies. Passes through the universe. This one could return. It doesn't always have to be. Somewhere else from where it started.

47. And while the volcanos boil. And the earth quakes. While the hurricanes pass

over everything like fire. She whispers. The words I want to hear. I see her mouth moving. While all the others. Are distracted. To tell me. She didn't know why she left. And that she wouldn't leave again. After seeing all the pain. It caused. A pain that, in the end, made no one better. Or smarter. Or wiser.

48. She could have stayed. When the carriage came. And watched it. From our bedroom window. The white bed with white sheets. The white walls and ceiling. The white lace curtains. And the feeling of rain. Early morning. There would have been no harm. In opening the window. To feel the breeze. From the passing carriage. As the horses. Pulled it by.

49. We might have learned everything. We needed to know from that. And that alone

might have spread. Inside our bodies. And deepened us. Given us enough of this life. To last us a lifetime. All that we saw. And heard. All that we felt. In that moment strained. By the blood and bone. By the beating heart. Of the unforgiving. And inhuman body. To make us more forgiving. More human. With ourselves. And each other.

v: opening

He opens the doors to an orange edge of light.

Breath rises from both.

The road is quiet.

As far as he can see.

He puts the lantern out.

Turns once to look at the empty stall.

And closes the doors.

kind to her

50. It's not always good. To know what comes next. People will say so. But what do they know? You could walk away. After we spend. A single day together. Never to see. Each other again. Morning is the eater. And eats all things. The destroyer. And destroys all things. All the words we said. And half-said. All the songs we sang. And half-sang. Half-drunk. The night before.

51. And so you go. And I go. To morning. And the new day. You in your chariot of sorrow. Pulled by two horses—remember and forget. And me on foot. With my feet. Of the same names. Slower than you. To do both. But when the horses rest. I'll have my chance. To catch up. To hear the words. You want to say. In the sun that

brightens the fields. In the rain. That gives the patinaed statues of men and women their tears.

52. In this year. Like every year. Of the dead. And of the living. Feted together. My apple tree. My broken branch. My rose bush. My plucked pink rosebud. The sun shines on both. The dark sky covers both. The clouds move on from both. But the horses never rest. Though I do get thirsty. And stop. At the nearest fresh-water stream. To drink. When my mouth gets dry. So I have to catch up to you. Again and again.

53. The carriage wheels dig. Deep grooves. In the mud. I draw a circle through the mudline. With a stick. Carve a fermata above the circle. A decrescendo there beneath. As the carriage carries your body

along the incomplete. Pentagram drawn. By the carriage wheels. In that space. On a road where. All the notes for a song. I imagine. Can't be written. Though I hear. Her humming. Through the carriage window.

54. The mud splattering my face. A small piece of mud particle. Obstructing the vision in one of my eyes. Because it flew into my pupil—a superficial penetration. And stayed there. Until a splash of water. From an unwieldy mud puddle. Washed it clear. But for a time. I used my memory. Vision for simple observation. Because my ordinary vision was hindered. For miles. And miles.

55. Though I could see into the carriage. With one eye. Like natural selection. Like a piano sonata for left hand. Played by an

unsteady right. As you lifted your dress to cool your ankles. And then a rest for your weary travels. To drink a plum aperitif. At a table by the river. The sun shining on your cheeks and temples.

56. Someone asked if you wanted to share a parasol. For the hot sun. Not yet setting on the horizon. You said no. But the terror of a parasol unopened. He used it to point to his little boat. Floating on the water. If I turned this way. I couldn't see it. And maybe soon enough. Forget about it altogether.

57. You clapped for him. And although I was put off. I loved your little clapping. Left hand over right. I blocked out every noise. To hear the little tapping. Of your fingers on your palm. As you moved on in the carriage. The moonlight shining through

the carriage window. Passing by the trees. Their calm but crooked branches. And lightly fanning leaves. Casting ever-changing masks upon your face. But always you. Your lips. Your eyes. Your nose. Your ears.

58. If I sat beside you. The coachman would pull me out. And throw me onto the road. How he'd see me I wouldn't know. I'd be well hidden. Tucked in among your clothes. But even if I knew. That briefest nuzzle—a few seconds of real history. Would still give me. The warmest feeling. Until my tumble near the carriage wheel.

59. I'd see a little girl watching. From the veranda. Her hands covering her ears. So she doesn't hear. The ruckus of the horses. The violence of the wheels.

Tomorrow she'll go into the forest. With her brother. To pick wild blueberries.

60. I tumble. To the river bank. And settle on my side. To see the river grass. And fallen yellow flowers. From the laburnum. Form fallen-yellow-flower streams. They disperse into the open water. I'll put a tree swing there. So the girl can swing. On sunny days. On rainy days. And if she's awake. When all the grown-ups sleep. On dark and quiet nights. She'll feel the river grass brush her feet. A lonely, little girl. Everyone should be kind to her.

61. Or one night someone will be sad. And think. There should be two of us here. Sitting on the veranda stairs. Watching the moon. Over the trees across the river. Two of us. Running into the house. To get out from the rain. Two of us examining.

The small tear. In your summer dress. Caught on the head. Of a loose veranda nail. And two of us in a carriage. Having a conversation. No one can hear.

62. And the boy racing us on his bicycle. Doesn't care. If the groceries in his bicycle basket. Fall out. He'll reach over. To give you an apple. Because of the way your hair. Moves in the wind. Outside the carriage window. Without ever being taught. He already seems to know. Before his turn. He'll stop and wave. As the carriage continues straight. Along the road. And without saying it. To each other. We'll think this is happiness.

63. I hope the boy thinks so too. Hugs his mother. When he gets home. Though he won't tell her what happened. He'll lie in bed at nights and remember. The sound of

his bicycle wheels on the road. How quickly the turn to his home approached. How he stood up to pedal. Faster and faster. And faster. His mother will notice. The missing groceries. But the way he hugged her. Happy and breathless. She'll put away what he brought back. And think about him. Like a sadness we're born with that we have to use.

64. If there was a bed in the carriage. I would fall asleep beside you. While you lie awake. And look up to the sky—our bedroom window. The blanket will cover. Only part of my grave. I won't know. If you stared. Tried to uncover. What's buried there. Or indifferent. Turned on your side. And looked away. When I wake up. You'll be gone. Like that summer. You cut your hair. Left all your

friends behind. And disappeared. They waved to you. But you didn't see them.

65. Was it carriage adventures? From baby carriage. To proper carriage. Those small things that happen. To quiet people. Who meet life. Where it is. In the unused backroom. In the untravelled alley. In the unexplored cave. They say the sun is a god. We say the shadow is life. And the sun. With all its might. Barely strong enough. To reveal it. I'll never forget you. Maybe you'll never forget me too. But I did. For a long time. Everyday a little more. Until today. I'm not sure. I remember anything real. About you at all.

66. But always elsewhere. How many ordinary days? And nights? Did you stand. Unmoved. How many ordinary words? Did you speak. Or did you? To ordinary people. Like me. On those

perfect. Sunny days you used. To hide all your ugly. And graceless labours. To create your beautiful. And graceful life.

67. I could only. Find you when I did. And exist with you. The way I do. Or never. Like the one-of-a-kind carriage-following shoes. I wear. To follow your carriage. All over the world. My body is the pine tree. And you. The dripping piece of honeycomb. Hanging without its hive. Deep inside my branches.

vi: beading

He pulls the cover away.

The wood is damp.

Beading small drops.

He wipes the sides.

The brass is dull.

From life.

The door latch holds firm.

panther lily

68. I search through. Old photographs of you. Maybe I'm in the background of one. Or two. I remember we were. In the same places sometimes. I think I see myself. But looking more closely. It's someone else. Though I'd wear. Those kinds of shirts and pants and belts. I might be. Just out of frame. When I recognize. A place. I've been before.

69. Me. Or the subatomic sense of me. Somewhere very close. I'll save those photographs of you. In the places I've also been. I could be. In the fitting room. Of the fancy shop adjacent. Under the stairs you're descending. In the distant airplane. Stopped by a camera click. Motionless above the trees. Or standing. On top of the carriage. Keeping my

balance. To conduct. The orchestra. Of clouds. Of birds. Of leaves. Of people unending. Of people unbending. Of people pretending.

70. All their colours. And sounds. And movements. We leave behind. Like notes on a measure. Of old sheet music. Over three-fourths time. Marching along. These roads. The worn-down bones. Of the places we pass through. Places we say. We'll never return to. But welcome us back. When we do. Even if we don't remember their names. Or the faces. Of the boys who sit. On the stone walls. They've aged. When we ride in.

71. Her hair falls over. The arm rest. Of the settee. Follows the curve. Of the fabric. To the floor. I'll climb a strand of her hair. Into her dreams. Or swing back and forth.

Higher and higher. In the perfumed air. To the ticking. Of the metronome. The clicking. Of the old stove. That won't light. And no match anywhere. To strike a fire.

72. We're in awe. Of how small. We are. In this. Big world. Keeping us around. Long enough. To love each other. Close our eyes. And if we're lucky. Say good-bye. Too many things. To miss. So many we can't think of them. But you and you and you. Most of all. There's an empty perfume bottle. On the dresser. It's been there since when. I can't remember. But when you open it. You'll feel sad.

73. And her dream: a cranium impulse and calculations of rain. A broken violin string. Like her hair. Someone's climbing the fingerboard (when she wakes up,

she'll think it's her). A crackle of stars. In her dream version of night. Bright only. Becoming dark. When the stars flash their light. Panther lily. The sun is the monster eye. Her soft and gentle eyelid. Bursts. Into blood-red petals. Through the carriage window. And onto the road. The lioness. The staircase. The carriage door.

74. The coachman opens it. For her. Locks it tight. Before I can approach. I'll climb on top again. And travel outside. But I can't be in. The birds. Or the wind. Can't be in. The butterflies. Can't be in. The sky. And the morning that wants. Quiet. Or the evening that wants. Quiet. Can't be in. The sun that begins to set. And disappears. The words we're saying. The words we've said.

75. Until silence. And we see the shapes. Of each other. In darkness. Like flowers.

Bloom at night. Through the chain-link fence. You, holding the watering can. Me, the butterfly net. Though I've never caught one. At night. I see them. Hanging under. Tree limbs. They don't have eyelids. It's just an object to have. In my hand. Like an empty suitcase. Or a hat. I'll never wear.

76. I can hang. On the underside. Of the carriage. Like one of them. When I'm resting. Butterflies need rest. From drinking nectar. All day. They could rest in my grave. The perfectly shaped rectangular prism. In the middle of my chest. And push through. The unmarked piece of fabric. The same colour. As my skin. When morning comes. To start a new day.

77. An evocation. Of my last breath. In the only world. I know. I feel it all. On this

last day. As I hang. From the carriage window. The leaves of the laburnum. Brushing my head and neck. A hard job. Being in it. Walking and crawling. We make our way. Living in this world. And searching. The grocery store. For a pomegranate.

78. Living in this world. And waiting for the train. Living in this world. And fighting sleep. Living in this world. And mispronouncing someone's name. Living in this world. And pushing buttons. That make machines beep. Living in this world. And laughing. Living in this world. And crying. Living in this world. And living. Living in this world. And dying.

79. Like butterflies. Become wisps of smoke. Take their place in the firmament. Over a

world. Spinning through the universe. Ephemera—filled with all the moments. Of a fleeting life. Too weighty. For the clouds. To hold. The earth can. Take them back. And the people who live there. The universe. Doesn't need them.

vii: falling

He rolls the carriage forward.

The wheels creak.

Then fall silent.

He aligns the shafts.

And fastens the traces.

The horse adjusts its stance.

And waits.

the history of an empire

80. We're not like. Those people. Who think. The world out there. Can save them. Grasses grow. From the dirt. Flowers too. Insects reveal themselves. Every day. Climb their stems and shoots. Sometimes fly off. While we move things. About in here. Lockets, photographs, candles. Boots. And move them back. So after what is done. No longer needs to be done.

81. And we can fall asleep. Among our books. *The History of an Empire*. Legions marching. Down your arm. *The Book of Lashonda*. On your shoulder. Sighing. Into your dreams. *One Note Symphonies*. A soft blanket. On your belly. The air accompanying. Its music. Moving softly. In and out. Of your lungs. You sleep as

beautiful as you are. And wake up to the day. As a flower. Opening to the sun.

82. As the carriage. Makes it way. Along these roads. A peek through. The carriage window. And she knows. She's almost there. Though some life. Between us. She can't remember. The past. Of that life. Belongs more to me. Than to her. Like the night. We sat. By the opened window. In the empty room. Above the crowded. Music hall below.

83. It's the corner. Of rooms. That seem to matter most. Later on now. Though we can't remember them. Later on. We'd like to. The photographs. And wooden bowl. Shaped like a linden leaf. Only deep enough. To hold two paper clips. On the small desk. And the small lamp. Rarely used. Its light. Lambent on the framed. Black and white. Of your mother and

father. When they were young. Leaning against the wall.

84. Like they might have leaned. Against a wall. When they were young. In the morning. You walk past it. Without looking. And days later. You won't remember that you wanted to. But I remember the corner. Of the empty room. Where I found you sitting. And I approached you. As I approach life. Never arriving. Or maybe. Arriving too late.

85. So that what I'm feeling. Is only the feeling. Of something impending. And not the thing itself. And then. I miss it. And I find myself. Approaching something else. It might have been better. If I tapped. A message. On the other side of the wall. In a secret code. Though it would have gotten lost. In the music. Still,

I could have told you. That's what I did later on.

86. Like insects warning us. That night is coming soon. And we must leave. These barren roads. For the darkness of the woods. You'll see the last light. Of the sun. Touch the carriage. As it disappears into the trees. And nocturnal animals disperse. Around it. Like grains of sugar from a sugar cube (in a cup of black coffee).

87. The trees tolerate us. As if we arrived too late. To the inn. Like an innkeeper disturbed. From his deep sleep. To light a candle. Place two pieces of bread. And a carafe of wine. On the table. He had already. Cleared away. But to see. Someone so beautiful. In front of him. Out of the blue.

88. All the elements. Of the moment. Are there: the bread, the wine, her face, her eyes, her hair. The wooden table and chairs. The single, lit candle. And the silence. Of the dark night. Coming through. The smallest spaces of the room. As the innkeeper. Stares at her. Before he leaves. Overcome by the moment. And the feeling it brings—a confirmation. That his time here is. After all. Something unique and unrepeatable.

89. He'll fall asleep with that moment. And she'll write. A short note. Thanking him. For his hospitality. Sign her name (Maria). At the bottom of the page. And lean the folded. Piece of paper. Against the empty glass. By the plate. Blow the candle out. Before she leaves. And when morning comes. The bright finger. Of the

sun. Will reach through. The opened window. To show him. The letter there.

90. Like it does. Through the trees. On this. Or that. Side of the carriage. As it wends its way. Through the natural paths. Of the woods. Leaves shimmer. In the first light. Of day. Morning stars. Replaced at night. Strangers take these roads. To go elsewhere. And sometimes. Kindred spirits meet. To share the illusion. Of something meaningful. They'll remember forever.

91. And these trees. Sensitive to the movements. Of people. And with great affection. For those. Who want to be. Left alone. Spy you. From their full length. Silently let you go. And if not silently. Then with that soft. And gentle breeze. From which one can infer. Like scientists

infer black holes. The dawn of a new day. Filled with possibilities.

92. But how quickly. Endless hope becomes. A thing of the past. And yet. The carriage goes on. Between those silent trees. And you with it. The princess of possibilities. Heir to the queen of possibilities. Daughter of the king of possibilities. And me your loyal subject. Who knows. How a beautiful human body. Moving through sunlit water. On a summer afternoon. Can be ugly. Earlier that day.

93. Her beauty. Makes my heart jump. Like a sparrow. To the top. Of the concrete steps. As the rest. Of the flock. Pecks at crumbs. Flung on the grass below. Then takes flight. To see. All of her. Circling but not knowing. Where to land. Like endless hope. More beautiful. To exhaust itself.

And float. Among the stars. Than fall and lie still. As if dead. Here on earth.

94. And in the carriage. As in her dark room. I'll lie still. On the floor. As she sleeps. On the bed orbiting. Around me. Like a planet. Where the atmosphere. Necessary for life. Exists. Where the faintest. Hint of breath. From her lungs. Resists. The end of all things. And provides enough air. For the barely living. To start again.

viii: hearing

He wipes the reins dry.

Buttons his coat.

And puts on his gloves.

The horse flicks its ear.

At a sound.

Only it can hear.

nightkeeper

95. The sun ascends. And the carriage moves slowly. Between the trees. I see a line. Of hedges. In the distance. And rising above them. On the hill. Like a forest flower. Growing above forest weeds (and is a weed itself). A steeple. I think I hear. The faint ringing. Of a bell. I think I see. People. Gather there. I hope the carriage. Goes a different way. Or they'll think. We're heading in that direction. Because of them.

96. I feel like I'm floating. In slow motion. Lying on the carriage top. As new leaves. On old branches. Fool me again. Brush my body. Clean of everything. It picked up. Before my carriage travels. Maria if it pleases you. I can shape tree bark. Into living rooms. Anything with the trees.

And you Maria. But if not. We'll keep going.

97. And the spring flowers. Pushing through. The forest soil. The tree branches reaching. For all corners. Of the earth. I hear the honeybees. Buzzing in the forest noise. They're going back. To the hive. To dance in the direction. Of the sun. All this commotion. All this chaos. But I can still see. In the gleaming eye. Of the blackbird. Watching quietly. From the forest tree. The silence and stillness. Of an ordered world.

98. The carriage moves. Into the clearing. And up a hill. Along a path that seems. To lead. To the top of the world. From where I can see. The world and the people. Of the world. Doing things. Hanging laundry. On the backyard. Clothesline. Spinning the bicycle wheel. To find the

puncture there. Wet socks. And lost keys. Too much. Of the too little. Life we get to live. But sometimes everything. Is in perfect balance. To give us a full dose. Of living.

99. The bicycle speeding. Us down the hill. Like free people. In the summer sun. The sheet rising. And falling. In the summer breeze. Hiding and unhiding us. Cooling our summer brow. Like the day. The little girl. Brought us something to drink. Tall enough now. To take the glasses. From the shelf. And turn the faucet on. We both remembered. How some spilled. When she came down. The veranda stairs.

100. But in a moment. Everything goes. Out of balance. Again Maria. We're riding past. The graveyard where. We bury. The people we love. And the day. The little girl left. I remember. How you told me.

She was gone. And you chasing after her. And me chasing after you. If I had fixed. The bicycle. It would have been easier. To keep up. You did. Tell me to. But I sat there. The wheel spinning. On the metal frame. Upside down. Staring. At the trees. Perfectly balanced. In the first morning. I woke up. And saw you both. Asleep.

101. I ran upstairs. But forgot. You too. Were gone. Left a book opened. On the bed. For me. Like a hole. In our garden fence. To another world. Of baby carriage. And proper carriage. Of horse and riding carriage. Of forests. And sugarcane fields. Of epochs. And cups of tea. Of graveyards. And galaxies. And of you. And you. And you. Most of all. I put my hand. Through the opening. Like a child. Thinking her hand. Might take mine. But felt only air.

102. But from up here. I see. The landscape beyond. The fence. To the forest. And the hill. Further away. And Maria. Leaning her head. Through the open carriage door. Taking in. The smell of salt. From the salty sea air. Looking back. At the small window. Atop the steeple. Where no stairs. Go. And yet. Someone could be. Watching. From up there. Taking notes. About what she saw. Between. The crowded sentences. Or in the empty margins. Of her book.

103. And further still. The clouds. Above the sea. The carriage. Heading there. I hold Maria's hand. Though she's really. Holding mine. She knows. I'm the one. Who's afraid. To take it. All in. Minuet, vase, pencil, chair. The quintillions. Of biological units. On planet Earth. More than. The number. Of galaxies. In the

observable universe. She'll push. Her hand. Through the grave. In the middle of my chest. And surprised. I'll say ouch. Though it wouldn't hurt.

104. And yet. I'll turn away. Because it might. And pretend to read. The letter. She wrote. To the innkeeper. Whom she mistakenly. Called the nightporter. Dearest nightporter. I thank you. For your kindness. Because she couldn't. Think of the word. Hospitality. Colder but more accurate. Though kindness did do. And would. Wherever and whenever. Such acts. As those rendered. By such people. As (mistakenly called by me) the nightkeeper. Are rendered.

105. And what more. She wrote. I hope your day. Tomorrow. Is profound. A word rarely used. In everyday conversation.

About the foreseeable future. And signed. Yours, In Good Memory. Maria. As if to leave. A record. For the people. Of the future. And for the future itself. About a time. When life. Was worth living. Even if no one cured. The worst diseases. Travelled to the limits. Of the universe. Or lived. For a thousand years.

ix: seeing

He mounts the seat.

The leather is cold.

The lantern gives enough light.

To see the road.

The horse's breath hangs in front.

a dark forgetfulness

106. A dark forgetfulness. The grave. And the people. Who lie there. But some tried. Before their end. In a word. In a note. In a drop of paint. Or piece of clay. In a graceful gesture. Of the arm. Though maybe. It can be enough. To score our names. And the years we lived. A postscript sent. Across time. And space. To the billions. Of years ago. When it all began. To say hello. To this. Great accident. In a language. Not yet formed.

107. Something smaller. Than an atom. Travelling through the void. Like the carriage. And Maria. A bright memory. Getting darker. Until one day. Those who owe her. Everything. Will never know. Where she was born. The parks. She played in. The sound. Of her voice. The

places. She lived. The people she loved. All she had to overcome. And in the end. Where she lay. Visited now. Only by the lost bird. Or the stray bee. Come far afield. To sip the nectar. From the flowers. Freshly planted. By those. Who clear the weeds. And brush the stones clean.

108. The last time. I visited. Was the year. The flowers didn't bloom. Everything grew green. From the strange light. And I don't know Maria. I was never. The same. Even when they. Bloomed again. The following spring. I was afraid. To touch them. Though I did. Pick one. A white dahlia. Dried and kept. As a bookmarker. In the book. You left. On the bed. Upstairs. And the story. In it. The random sentences. I read. Felt like destiny.

109. And lingering there. I made out. From the commotion. Of birds outside. A melody. I couldn't stop. Playing in my head. All day. I played it over. And over again. Before I fell asleep. And dreamed. Everything I told. Myself to dream. And again. The following night. In my head. I played the melody. Like a key. And dreamed. Everything I told. Myself to dream. Of the future. And you. And the girl. Picking strawberries. In the garden. While I made us tea.

110. But I woke up. And felt my heart. Hurting. So suddenly. And after so much time. I played the melody. In my head. Before I fell asleep. And dreamed everything. I told myself. To dream. This time. Of the past. And you. And the girl. Picking strawberries. In the garden. While I made us tea.

111. And woke up again. Still. Loosely bound. By sleep. To find a grave. In the middle of my chest. Where my beating heart. Used to be. And my head empty. Of all melodies. Of all dreams. Or I would have stayed. In that room. Forever. To live. Without the sadness. Of your absence. Is to live. Without the vastness. Of the sky.

x: departing

He opens the gate to the house.

The hinges groan.

He sees the figure of a woman.

Through the fog.

The horse lifts its head.

He shuts the carriage door.

And climbs up again.

He hears her voice from inside.

Go on.

And then the first turn.

Of the carriage wheels.

our simple biology

112. If there. Were the possibility. Of return. I'd return. As a breeze. Cruising down. Mountain slopes. Along ocean waves. Across continents. And countries. Over the tops of trees. And down. To the roads. You've travelled. To lift loose. Pigeon feathers. Into the air. Tussle the horse's mane. Sway the coachman's reins. Then into the carriage. To softly. Move across. Your face and hair. So you close. Your eyes and feel. In that moment. Your whole life. Then circle the earth. To return to you again.

113. Perhaps your journey. Would have ended. And I'd find you. While you slept. And perhaps. Sleeping. You'd sense my presence. As the carriage stops. And you wake. Up to the sea. Eyes half-opened.

Searching clouds. On the horizon. Waking from. Their afternoon sleep. Each taking. Its own way. As you piece together. Images of the dream. You dreamed. Of the boy. Chasing the carriage. On his bicycle. Turned down a road. Disappeared. Into the trees.

114. Then rest your head. On my shoulder. As you find. The strength. To be awake. And finding it. Look through. The carriage window. To the sea. And breathe. The salty sea air. Turn to find me. But I'm not there. Fallen behind. Suspended on a tree limb. One hand stuck. As if in the past. Still in mid-air. While the other hand. Searches. For another limb. To swing. My body. To a future. Half of me. Doesn't want. To live in. Not thinking. Half of me. Is the whole thing.

115. You tell. The coachman. To stop the carriage. The horses nibble on. Patches of grass. In the sand. As great forces. Of the world. Meet on the horizon. You want. To go home. I hear two. Clicking sounds. The carriage. Turns around. It's the same. When someone dies. As when. They are born. How did they. Find the strength. To do anything. In the days. After to breathe. To walk. To think. To live.

116. But we do. Breathe. And walk. To the kitchen. To the cup. To the spoon. To the empty bowl. A few days ago. Filled with sugar cubes. And stand there. By the sink. And think. About living. And live. Our simple biology. The carriage turns. Towards me. I let go. And fall. Like a bird. Forgetting how to fly. Falls through a tree. And on top. Of the carriage again. Looking forward. To the sea gulls. Flying

above. The sea sprays. As the carriage. Takes us back.

117. I hope it. Takes us back. A different way. Or people will think. We're heading. In that direction. Because of them. To the steeple. Slipping by. The woman who takes notes. In between the sentences. And margins. Of her book. As she sleeps. So she won't write. About what she sees. Because I can't penetrate. Her gaze. As she looks down. From up there. To let her know. Put your pencil down Maria (if that were her name). And take it all in.

118. I mumbled all night. From exhaustion anyway. Until the birds woke up. And wouldn't have seen her. Even if her eyes. Sparkled at night. In whatever colour they were. And now. Every little thing. Mumble mumble. Every small thing.

Mumble mumble. Every infinitesimal thing. Mumble mumble. Disconnected-once-again-connected. Might be. The only happiness. We know.

xi: returning

He returns before dark.

The horse is tired and calm.

He unhitches the traces.

And removes the harness.

Hangs it on its hook.

The wheels are streaked with mud.

And he takes his time.

To wipe them clean.

Inside the carriage.

He finds a strand of hair.

Where the woman leaned her head.

To sleep.

it was all

119. I fell asleep. On the carriage top. And dreamt. We spoke. As two people. Who wanted to say. Something to each other. We could never. Find the words for. But in the dream. Did say the words. We wanted to hear. Told each other. Everything in words. We had never said. Or heard awake.

120. And when I woke up. I thought you might. Have had the same. Dream and I tried. To find something. In the world. Around you. That would show me. You did. Maybe you'd reach. Through the carriage window. And let. Your arm. Hang over. The door. Even if it rained. Or stopping by a stream. Put your shoes. Next to mine. If we put our feet in. Gently

kick the water. To cause a little splash. And make it. Clear.

121. Or maybe. You would have the dream. The next night. Or the night after. Or sometime later. The next year. Or the year after. And you'd search. The world around me. For something that would. Show you. I had dreamed. The same dream. And said everything. You wanted. To say. And heard everything. You wanted to hear. But it would be. Too late. To know. And we would. Miss each other. Even though I did.

122. The carriage. Rumbled on. And we passed one tree. Then another. Until after. Passing thousands. We stopped. At the edge. Of the woods. From where. I could see. Her house. And the window. To her room. And from where. She could see. To

the trees. And I wondered. How many times. As she was falling. Asleep looked at them. As friends always. Nearby to spend. Time with her. Before the end.

123. Of the day. Maybe there was one. Growing. On the same sad. Ground on which. All her flowers grew. Even her happiness. And on days. When nothing grew. Left her. To till the dirt. And plant the seeds. That might grow. The flowers. To cover it. She could pick one. Or two. Wash the stems clean. And give them. To the people. She loved. So they would. Have something. Beautiful from her.

124. Sometimes she would sing. Or hum. And her melody. Would drift. Through the opened window. So anyone passing. By would hear. Something in a voice. That made them pause. And think there was. Someone beautiful. Up there. And

for a moment. Forgetting everything. Believe one day. Beauty would be enough. And when. She stopped. And there. Was silence. They would be mistaken. To think it. Was only that.

125. Before remembering. The package. They were delivering. And continue. On their way. But I stopped. And this. Is how we started. She's up there. Trying to gather. Everything leaking out. The first memory. The second. The hundred-and-twenty-third. The thousand-and-fifty-first. The name he gave. His bicycle. The song she played. On her clarinet. The day she. Wept when he left. She could use. The grave dug. Into the middle. Of my chest. To catch anything. That slipped through. Her brain.

126. I see. The carriage. Pulling in. At the front. Door maybe. She hears. The

clopping of the horses. On the cobble stone. I'm looking. For her shadow. In the room. But I don't see it. Anymore or hear. Her song. She's probably taken. The stairs. To the first floor. And called out. So softly. No one. Can hear. But she had left them all. While she was still asleep.

127. I'll jump down. From the fence. And make my way. Across the open. Field through the light. Of the morning breeze. The small wildflowers. Dotting the grass. To the side. Of her house. And climb. The ivy trellis. Into her room. The door. Slightly ajar. I see her float. Down the stairs. Like a ghost. Or was I seeing things.

128. I watched her. From up there. As she moved. From room to room. And stopped. At the photograph. Of the grave. That if

taken. From further away. Would have shown. My body stretched. Out on a field. With a perfectly shaped rectangular. Prism in the middle. Of my chest. My eyes closed. To this place. The lines. On my face. An epitaph. To a beloved. Biological unit. Living somewhere else.

129. The room. Of future ruins. The candle holder. The small side table. The lamp. Tumbled over. The picture. And picture frame. Dug up. By the little girl. Whose family. Recently moved in. Trampled on. By the trucks. That rolled. Back and forth. To build a new room. For her to sleep in. With a window. To the trees. The history. Of the metal. Of the plastic. Of the untied. Shoelaces. On the shoes. The boy in the photograph wore. And the history. Of him.

130. It was all. She could bear.

www.ingramcontent.com/pod-product-compliance
Lightning Source LLC
Chambersburg PA
CBHW031354160426
43196CB00007B/811